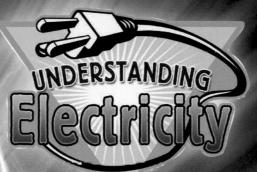

Understanding Electricity

What Are Insulators and Conductors?

Jessica Pegis

Crabtree Publishing Company

www.crabtreebooks.com

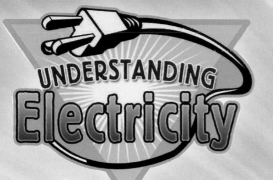

IMPORTANT
All experiments in this book can
be conducted by children. When
working with electricity, however, it
is always recommended that children
work with adult supervision.

Author: Jessica Pegis
Publishing plan research and development:
Sean Charlebois, Reagan Miller
Crabtree Publishing Company
Project development: Clarity Content Services
Project management: Karen Iversen
Editors: Rachel Eagen, Francine Geraci
Proofreader: Kathy Middleton
Photo research: Linda Tanaka
Design: First Image
Cover design: Margaret Amy Salter, Ken Wright
Production coordinator: Ken Wright
Prepress technician: Ken Wright
Print coordinator: Katherine Berti

Illustrations:
Chandra Ganegoda

Photographs:
cover shutterstock; p1 azaphoto/shutterstock; p4
Jupiterimages/Thinkstock; p5 shutterstock; p6 Eldred
Lim/shutterstock; p7 (top) Angela Waye/shutterstock,
(bottom) Max Topchii/shutterstock; p8 iStockphoto/
Thinkstock, Nikola Bilic/shutterstock; p9 top Rob kemp/
shutterstock, iStockphoto/shutterstock; p10 (top) redfrisbee/
shutterstock, (bottom) andrey_l/shutterstock; p11 (top)
remik44992/ shutterstock, (bottom) auremar/ shutterstock;
p12 George Doyle/Thinkstock; p14 Krivosheev Vitaly/
shutterstock; p15 Jag_cz/shutterstock; p16 top DrMadra/
shutterstock, Lusoimages/shutterstock; p17 top Losevsky
Pavel/ shutterstock, Yurchyks/shutterstock; p18 Jorg
Hackemann/shutterstock; p19 iStockphoto/Thinkstock; p20
wavebreakmedia ltd/shutterstock; p21 Diego Cervo/
shutterstock; p22 top clearviewstock/shutterstock, SPbPhoto/
shutterstock; p23 emin kuliyev/shutterstock; p24 top Hadi
Djunaedi/ shutterstock, Vladimir Mucibabic/ shutterstock; p25
top Texasdex/GNU license wiki, Rainer Plendl/ shutterstock;
p26 top omer cicek/shutterstock, Ma0-Linh Doan/CCL/wiki;
p27 John Foxx/Thinkstock; p28 Image originally created by
IBM Corporation; p29 Babich Alexander/shutterstock.

Library and Archives Canada Cataloguing in Publication

Pegis, Jessica
    What are insulators and conductors? / Jessica Pegis.

(Understanding electricity)
Includes index.
Issued also in electric format.
ISBN 978-0-7787-2078-2 (bound).--ISBN 978-0-7787-2083-6 (pbk.)

    1. Electric conductors--Juvenile literature. 2. Electric insulators
and insulation--Juvenile literature. 3. Electricity--Juvenile literature.
I. Title. II. Series: Understanding electricity (St. Catharines, Ont.)

TK3311.P45 2012   j621.319'3   C2012-901508-3

Library of Congress Cataloging-in-Publication Data

CIP available at Library of Congress

Crabtree Publishing Company
www.crabtreebooks.com   1-800-387-7650

Printed in Canada/042012/KR20120316

Published in Canada
Crabtree Publishing
616 Welland Ave.
St. Catharines, ON
L2M 5V6

Published in the United States
Crabtree Publishing
PMB 59051
350 Fifth Avenue, 59th Floor
New York, New York 10118

Published in the United Kingdom
Crabtree Publishing
Maritime House
Basin Road North, Hove
BN41 1WR

Published in Australia
Crabtree Publishing
3 Charles Street
Coburg North
VIC 3058

Contents

Turn It On!

You use electricity every day. Electricity powers your home, and many of your favorite gadgets. All you need to do is turn them on.

What Is Electricity?

All matter is made of **atoms**, and each atom has a proton, a neutron, and electrons. Protons have a positive (+) electrical charge. Neutrons have no charge. Electrons have a negative (–) charge. Opposite charges are attracted to each other. Electricity forms when there is a buildup of one kind of charge—usually a negative one.

Electricity can be static, which means many particles with the same charge stick together but do not move. Electricity can also move. An electrical **current** results when many electrons move in one direction.

When a machine is turned on, electrons are pushed out by a power source, such as a battery or **generator**. The electrons move through a **conductor**, such as copper wire, and into the machine to make it run.

You use electricity in so many ways throughout the day. Electricity helps make life convenient and fun.

Can Electricity Flow Through Everything?

While a current flows through an electrical appliance, it does not shock you. Try the investigation on the next page to see why.

Try It for Yourself!

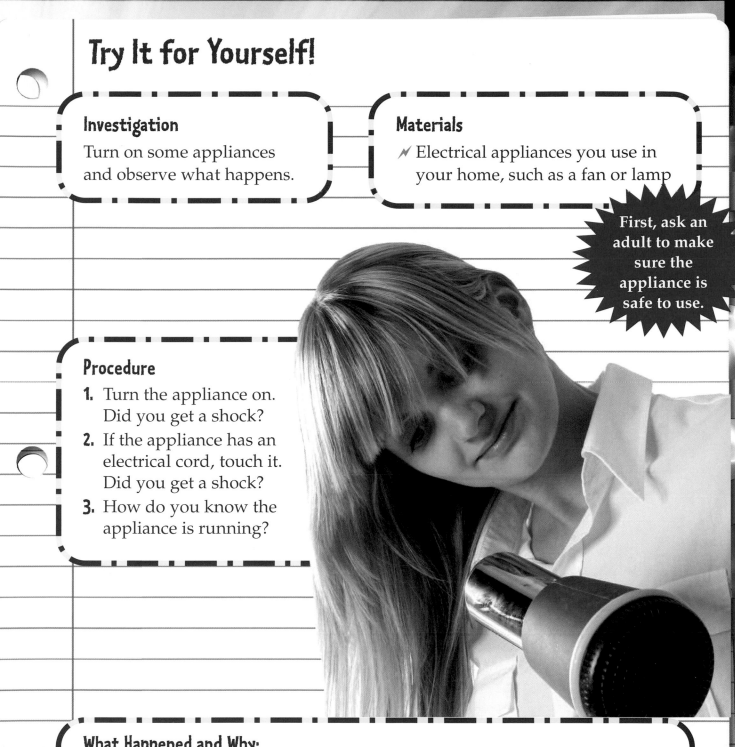

First, ask an adult to make sure the appliance is safe to use.

Investigation

Turn on some appliances and observe what happens.

Materials

⚡ Electrical appliances you use in your home, such as a fan or lamp

Procedure

1. Turn the appliance on. Did you get a shock?
2. If the appliance has an electrical cord, touch it. Did you get a shock?
3. How do you know the appliance is running?

What Happened and Why:

When you turned on the appliance and touched the cord, you did not get a shock. You know the appliance is running because you can see or feel some type of energy. The switch and the cord are protecting you from electricity. They are **insulators**. The electrons are running through a wire inside the cord. The wire is a conductor, but the covering on the cord is an insulator.

Conductors and How They Work

Conductors are materials that electricity can easily pass through.

Electrons Just Want to Be Free

Not every material is a good conductor of electricity. The best conductors have electrons that are always ready to escape their atoms. That is what makes copper one of the best conductors. Copper atoms have 29 electrons, and one of them is always free. As soon as the power is switched on, the free copper electrons can be directed along a path. They flow through a machine or appliance to make it run. Many homes are strung with copper wiring that delivers electricity to every room.

Copper is an excellent conductor. This copper wiring can be used in plumbing, heating, or air-conditioning systems in homes.

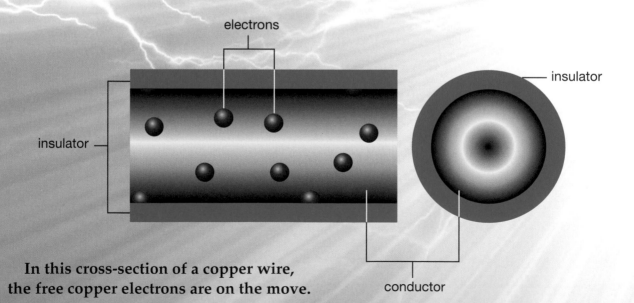

electrons

insulator

insulator

conductor

In this cross-section of a copper wire, the free copper electrons are on the move.

Why Are Metals Good Conductors?

Most metals are good conductors. Their atoms usually have one electron that can escape easily and start a current. Gold is an excellent conductor. It does not **corrode**, or break down, over time. Gold is expensive, however, so it is not practical for use as household wiring.

Silver is the best conductor of all the metals—better than copper—but it is also expensive, and it can **oxidize**. That means its chemistry changes when it is exposed to oxygen, which is in air. Silver is sometimes used as a conductor in satellites because there is no oxygen in space to harm the silver.

Silver may be used as a conductor in satellites that orbit Earth. Unlike other metals, silver ensures an even conductivity of current.

A tiny amount of gold is often used as a conductor in USB cables. These cables connect your computer to other devices such as a flash drive. Gold ensures maximum conductivity.

Insulators and How They Work

Insulators are materials that electricity cannot pass through.

No Electron Excitement

Unlike conductors, insulators are materials without free electrons. They also resist becoming charged by electrons that are introduced from an outside source, such as a battery or generator. Think of an insulator as a boring party guest. It cannot produce the electron excitement needed to create an electric current. Insulators are useful because they let you touch and use electrical appliances, without coming into contact with the electrical current that makes them run.

Insulators have **resistance** to electrical current. That means they do not allow electrical current to pass through them. Resistance is measured in **ohms**. The greater the number of ohms, the greater the material's resistance to electrical current.

Like people, electrons need the right conditions to get excited and move around. Insulators prevent electrons from moving from one atom to another.

Can you spot the insulator? If you guessed the colorful rubber tubes, you are correct. The copper wiring inside is insulated with rubber to make it safe for handling and to keep the current contained.

Flash fact

The ohm is named for its inventor, Georg Simon Ohm (1789–1854), a German high school teacher who went on to become a great physicist.

What Are Some Good Insulators?

Rubber and plastic are two of the best insulators. That is why electrical cords and electrical wiring are covered in material made of rubber or plastic. Glass and ceramic, which is clay hardened by heat, are also good insulators.

You have probably seen utility poles in your neighborhood. They are the tall, wooden poles that have wires that stretch to other poles along the street. The next time you see one, look for the bumpy notches near the top. These bumps are insulators. They ensure that electricity does not leak out of the pole and harm people or the environment.

The glass insulators are the round, green disks on this utility pole.

Flash fact

Glass insulators were first made in the 1800s. They come in lots of colors and shapes, and are a fun collectible today!

Conductors and Insulators Everywhere

Conductors and insulators make life convenient by providing safe electrical current.

Current Events

Electrical current powers all types of home appliances and technology, from electric can openers to televisions. In some appliances, electrical current acts as a heater. For example, the burners on an electric stove conduct electricity in order to heat up. Burners are coils of nichrome made of nickel and chromium. Toasters and hair dryers also use nichrome as a conductor to create heat.

Always make sure that you touch electric appliances where they are insulated. It is safe to turn the plastic knobs on your stove or to hold your hair dryer at the base. For safety reasons, you should never touch the electrical element, such as the coils inside a hair dryer, when an electric device is running.

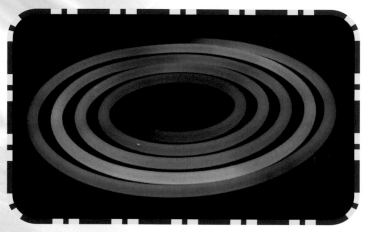

The nichrome burner on an electric stove heats up as it conducts electricity.

By keeping your hands on the insulating base of a hair dryer, you can avoid getting an electric shock or burning yourself.

Flash fact

The filament, or wire, in a traditional light bulb is a conductor, but provides more heat than light. That is why traditional light bulbs are not very energy-efficient.

Conductors and Insulators Outdoors

Conductors and insulators help provide electricity in a safe way to your community. Electricity powers the traffic lights while plastic insulators cover the cables that carry the power. Streetlights guide your way but are well insulated from top to bottom to prevent injury to people and workers.

People who work with electricity must wear insulating clothing to protect themselves from electric shock. This clothing must cover the whole body. The buttons must be made of a non-conductive material, such as plastic. Protective hats and footwear must also be worn at all times.

This electrician is wearing insulating gloves while working with electrical wiring.

Conductors and insulators are at work when you cross the street at a pedestrian crossing.

11

Conductor or Insulator?

Try It for Yourself!

Experiment

Using a simple circuit that you build, test materials you collect to see if they are conductors or insulators.

Materials

- small objects from your home or school, such as paper clips, small wooden items, fabric, erasers, coins, keys
- D battery
- miniature light bulb and base
- 3 pieces of 18- to 22-gauge copper wire

You might have some D batteries on hand because they are used in many flashlights. You can buy the bulb, wire, and clips at a hardware store.

Procedure

1. Sort the objects you collected into two groups: the objects that you think will be good conductors and the objects you think will be good insulators.
2. With an adult, build a simple circuit following these steps:
   - Strip about 1 inch (2.5 cm) of insulation from the ends of the copper wire.
   - Attach one end of the wire to the positive end of the battery. Look closely at the battery. One end has a positive (+) symbol and the other end has a negative (−) symbol. If you do not have clips like the ones shown in the illustration, you can use tape to secure the wire to the battery.
   - Connect the other end of the wire to one side of the miniature light bulb base. (The base should have two tiny arms or loops to which you can attach a wire.)
   - Attach a second wire to the negative side of the battery.
   - Attach a third wire to the other arm of the miniature light bulb base.

Continue with the procedure on the next page.

Procedure

3. Test the objects in each group by connecting the two free ends of wire to each object.

4. Observe each time whether the bulb lights up or not.

5. Sort your objects again, this time according to which ones made the bulb light up and which did not.

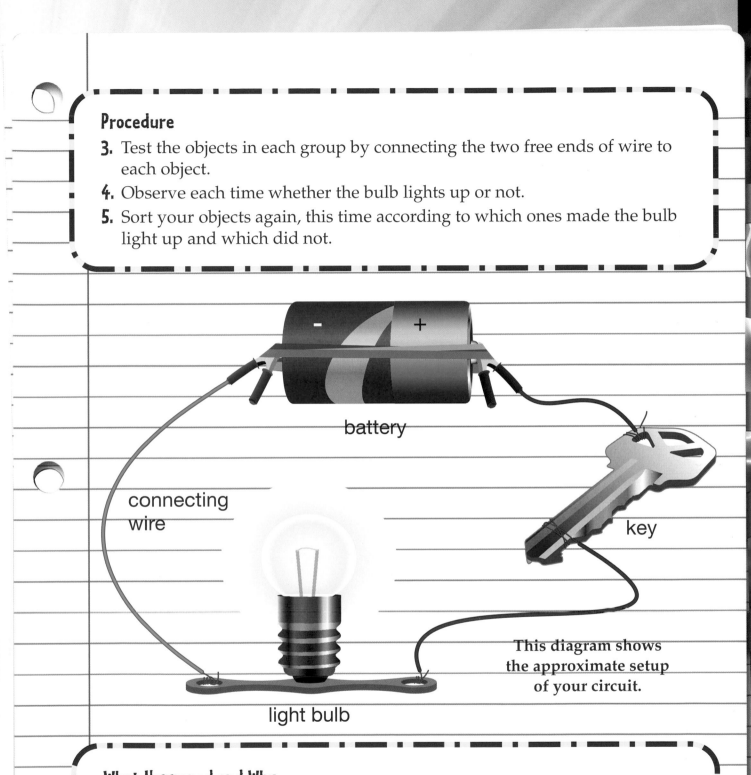

battery

connecting wire

key

light bulb

This diagram shows the approximate setup of your circuit.

What Happened and Why

Some objects made the light bulb light up, and some did not. The ones that did are good conductors of electricity. The ones that did not are good insulators. Were your original guesses about which objects would make good conductors and insulators correct? What did you learn from this experiment?

Lightning!

Lightning occurs because positive and negative charges have been separated in the atmosphere. When these charges line up, they discharge an awesome spark called static.

Outdoor Dangers

Lightning can be dangerous. In North America, hundreds of people are struck by lightning each year. They are usually struck outdoors, in an open space or when standing next to a tree. If lightning strikes a tree, it can "jump" to a person nearby or travel to the ground and become a ground current. Anyone walking nearby can be injured from this current.

During a storm, you can protect yourself from lightning by going inside a building with a **lightning rod**.

Lightning provides a beautiful display of color and light, but you are safer viewing it from indoors.

Flash fact

Lightning is so hot, it can heat up the air around it to five times the temperature of the sun.

Protection Against Lightning

A lightning rod is a giant conductor of lightning. Although that may sound strange, lightning rods work by redirecting the lightning safely into the ground.

Lightning rods that sit on top of buildings are made of copper or some other conductive material. As lightning passes through the rod, it travels down a wire and into the ground, where the electrical charge weakens and scatters.

Airplanes have a unique way of protecting passengers from lightning. Most planes are made of aluminum, which is a good conductor. However, when lightning strikes the plane, the electricity passes along its aluminum surface, then just flows away.

lightning rod (conductor)

wire

ground rod

The lightning rod conducts the lightning safely into the ground through a wire that runs inside the building.

Lightning travels across the conductive surface of a plane but does not harm it.

The Electrifying Third Rail

Trains, including railway trains and subways, need electric power to run.

Running Power

How do they get this power? Often it comes from the **third rail**. The third rail is a giant conductor that runs alongside the train track and provides a continuous current of electricity. Power comes from an outside source connected to the train system with cables. A special device transfers the current to the train's electric motor to make it run.

In this picture the third rail is the dark rail that runs along the side of the main track.

A streetcar, or trolley car, is another type of vehicle that needs electric power to run. It receives its electric current through overhead lines.

This streetcar gets its electricity from the wire above it. A device called a trolley pole collects the current from the wire and sends it to the streetcar to make it run.

Third Rail Safety

The third rail is dangerous because of its powerful electrical current. Anyone who touches it can be electrocuted. When someone falls against the third rail, the human body acts as a conductor. It sends the electrical charge into the ground just like a lightning rod. Birds or rodents who come in contact with the third rail do not have this problem because they are small and cannot be on the ground and the rail at the same time.

Because the third rail is so dangerous to humans, it is never on the platform side of the train. If someone accidentally falls into the track, contact with the third rail is mostly avoided.

It is always a good idea to stand back from the edge of a subway platform.

Flash fact

In 1906 the toymaker Lionel Corporation became the first company to add a third rail to its toy train, resulting in the first electric train.

Water: Conductor or Insulator?

You may have already heard that it is unsafe to mix water and electricity. Does this mean that water is a conductor?

All in the Particles

Would you be surprised to learn that water can be either a conductor or an insulator? It all depends on the purity of the water.

Ordinary water is a good conductor. This is because water that you drink from a glass or see in a rain puddle contains impurities. Impurities in water are electrically charged particles, or tiny pieces of matter, such as salt and metal **ions**. When electrons flow into this water they start a current. It is the impurities that conduct the electricity, not the water.

Charged particles are also present in the water that is in your body. Since the human body is 70 percent water, it makes an excellent conductor.

There is more than meets the eye to a glass of tap water.

Moisture on your skin will increase your ability to conduct electricity! Make sure your hands are dry and that you are not standing in any water when using electricity.

Pure Water vs. Ordinary Water

While ordinary water is a conductor, pure water is an insulator. By themselves, water **molecules**, or bunches of atoms, will not excite any electrons. Pure water takes time to make, however, and it does not stay pure. As soon as you leave pure water out in the air, it stops being pure. For this reason, pure water is used in only very controlled conditions, such as in machines that sterilize medical or dental instruments.

A small amount of pure water is also used in car batteries. Water mixed with sulphuric acid causes lead plates inside the battery to release electrons in order to produce electricity. Water must be pure so that it will not interfere with the battery's production of electricity.

Electricity from a car battery starts the engine and powers the windshield wipers and car radio. Pure water inside the battery helps to prolong the battery's life.

Air: Conductor or Insulator?

You cannot touch air and you can see right through it. Yet air must be either a conductor or an insulator.

Air Protection

In fact, air is a good insulator! Think about it for a minute. If air was a good conductor, it would be difficult to control any electric current. Everything around us would have to be insulated so as not to produce a spark. Electric lights and appliances would be dangerous to operate or to keep in your home.

Air molecules are too far apart to conduct any electricity. When molecules are far apart, they are less likely to become excited. Even power lines rely mostly on air as an insulator because it is too expensive to coat every power line in plastic.

If air was not an insulator, you would not be able to sit in your home and enjoy that movie on television safely.

Air as a Conductor

Air is an excellent insulator, but it can become a conductor under certain conditions. One way is when lightning occurs. Lightning is a huge discharge of electricity into the air. This discharge is strong enough to coax electrons out of their molecules. When the electrons are free to move about, air is capable of conducting electricity.

Air also acts as a conductor when there is an **electrical arc**. This is an electrical current moving from one solid conductor to another through a gas such as air. The air becomes charged much the way it does when there is lightning.

Electrical arcs are used by welders to melt metals together when making machinery and other manufactured goods. The intense heat and light from the electrical arc can be dangerous, so workers must wear protective gear at all times.

air

shrapnel

intense light and heat

conductor 1   conductor 2

As the current moves from one conductor to the other, there is a burst of light and heat, similar to lightning. This can make fragments of the solid conductor (shrapnel) break off.

Sparks fly as a welder uses an electrical arc in a steel factory. Special gear protects the welder's skin and eyes from injury.

The Mighty Vacuum

There is still something that makes a better insulator than air. What do you think it is? It is no air at all. No matter at all.

Zero Particles

The absence of matter is called a **vacuum**. In theory, a vacuum contains zero particles of matter, which should make it a good insulator. Without atoms, there is nothing to conduct any energy in the form of heat or electricity. Air vacuums are sometimes used as insulators in buildings because they stop the conduction of heat.

But that is not the end of the story. A vacuum can conduct electricity under certain conditions. Scientists explain it this way: When the electrical force is extremely high, nothing can stop electrons from flowing. When electrons are pushed by a mega-force between a positive (+) and a negative (–) terminal, they will flow even in a vacuum. In other words, with enough force, electrons will create their own conductor.

Outer space is a large vacuum, but it does contain atoms. They are too far apart, however, to conduct much electricity.

For years, vacuum tubes were used in radios, televisions, and other appliances. Electrons were pushed with great force through a vacuum to make these machines run.

How Are Air Vacuums Used?

Air vacuums have many uses in medicine, science, and industry. For example, air is vacuumed out of the traditional light bulb when it is manufactured. If the air were not removed, the metal filament that lights up would get damaged and burn out quickly.

An air vacuum is also required in the electron microscope. This powerful type of microscope uses electrons to magnify a sample. In order to preserve the powerful electron beam that creates the image, the sample must be viewed within a vacuum. Otherwise, air molecules could excite and scatter the electrons, which would distort the image.

Electron microscopes are about 5,000 times more powerful than standard light microscopes. They are large because they require a high-quality vacuum system to make them operate.

What Are Semiconductors?

Semiconductors **are materials that are halfway between a conductor and an insulator.**

Stop and Go

Semiconductors can conduct electricity and also resist the flow of electricity. Their ability to both conduct and insulate makes them very useful. Semiconductors can let electricity through or stop it, like a switch. A semiconductor can also increase the power of an electrical signal.

Before the computer age, semiconductors were used in transistor radios and hearing aids. Their compactness, along with their ability to amplify sound, was a technology breakthrough in the 1950s.

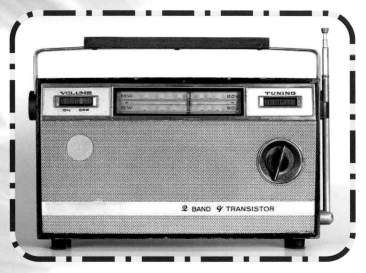

The transistor radio was the first radio that was small enough to be easily carried around. By today's standards, it was still very big!

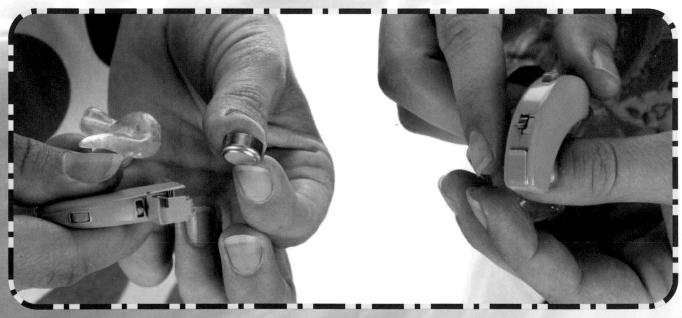

Semiconductors are used in hearing aids to increase sound.

Semiconductors and the Computer Revolution

Semiconductors are used in most electronic devices. In many ways, they are responsible for the digital age. Before semiconductors, computers had bulky vacuum tubes that controlled the flow of electrical current. The world's first electronic computer had 19,000 vacuum tubes and filled an entire room! It was made by the United States Army. Computers are now much smaller in design. They have become very important around the world.

The first computer was called ENIAC, short for Electronic Numerical Integrator And Computer.

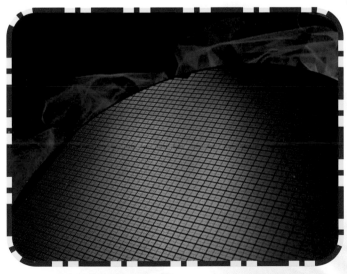

More than a dozen of these microchips would fit on the end of your index finger. All the microchips in a computer would not weigh more than 2.5 ounces (72 grams) altogether.

Then came the **microchip**—a thin wafer of semiconductive material packed with circuitry. The microchip is the brain of the modern computer or any computerized device, such as a clock or calculator. The electrical current controlled by the semiconductor enables the computer to perform all its tasks. The microchip paved the way for the ultra-fast and compact computers of today.

Flash fact

Silicon Valley in California got its name from silicon—a chemical element used to make the microchip. Silicon Valley is home to many microchip inventors and manufacturers.

What Are Superconductors?

Superconductors **are materials that have no resistance to electric current.**

Super Cool

Even good conductors have some resistance to electrical current. Energy is used to overcome this resistance and is released as heat. Constant heating means the conductor eventually gets damaged. Superconducting ability occurs when some conductors are subjected to very low temperatures—lower than –450°F (–232°C). In this state, their electrical resistance drops to zero. They can conduct an electrical current for as long as needed with no loss of energy.

Aluminum and mercury are two conductors that become superconductors when cooled. Ceramic—clay hardened by heat—is also a superconductor at very cold temperatures. Scientists are trying to find a way to get superconductors to work without extreme cooling, which is an expensive and time-consuming process.

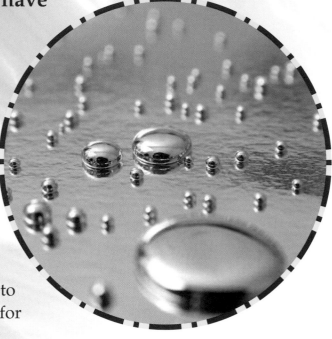

Mercury is a liquid metal at standard air temperature. It becomes a solid at –38°F (–39°C) and a superconductor when cooled to below –450°F (–232°C).

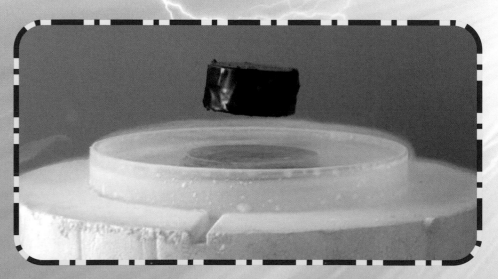

This is no magic trick! The current that flows on the surface of this cooled superconductor has enough power to push this magnet away. In the future, spacecraft may be able to hover over the surface of planets using this technology.

How Are Superconductors Used?

Superconductors are used in a number of specialized fields. A magnetic resonance imaging (MRI) machine uses a superconducting magnet to take detailed pictures of the inside of the human body. The magnet must be cooled constantly, using liquid helium and nitrogen, to protect it. To retain the cold and prevent damage to the machine, the magnet and its cooling system are insulated by a vacuum.

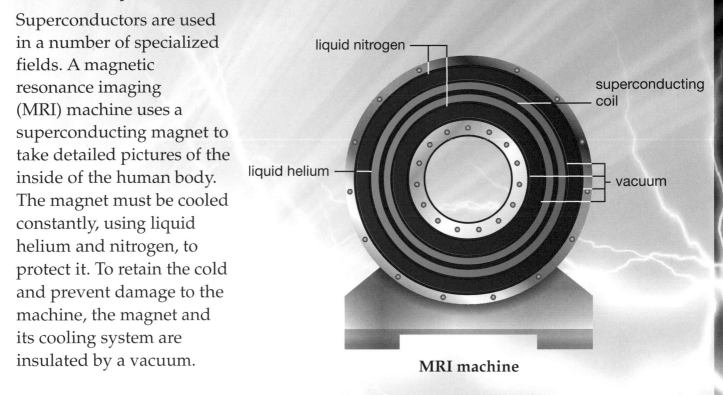

liquid nitrogen

superconducting coil

liquid helium

vacuum

MRI machine

Superconductors are also used in some generators and motors. Electrical generators built with superconducting wire are much more efficient than regular generators. However, the wires must be kept cold, which is expensive to do.

Physicians use MRI machines to diagnose many conditions, including digestive, heart, brain, bone, and muscle problems.

What Is Next for Conductors and Insulators?

Scientists are always researching ways that we can make better insulators and conductors.

Smaller, Faster, Mightier

In computer technology, microchips are getting smaller and more powerful, with circuits more than a thousand times smaller than a human hair. Scientists say that smaller chips are also more efficient because they leak less power.

In physics, a new type of electron microscope, called the Scanning Tunneling Microscope, is so precise that it can display the image of an atom.

In medicine, scientists are working to make MRI units with superconductors that do not need cooling. One day, MRI technology could be much less costly and even portable. Patients could be scanned in an ambulance before they arrive at the hospital.

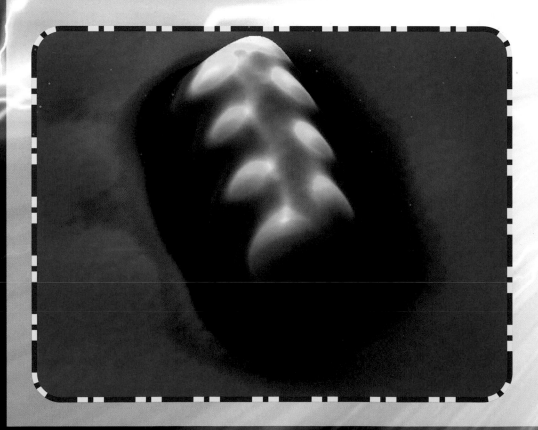

This image of a molecule containing the metal cesium and iodine on copper, was captured by the Scanning Tunneling Microscope.

Now, That Is Flashy!

How about paint that can be turned "on" or "off" to conduct either heat or electricity? Or printer ink that can hold conductors, semiconductors, and insulators so that you could create and "print" your own electronics?

These are just some of the latest ideas in the world of conductors and insulators. Carbo e-Therm is a coating made of carbon and graphite. The company that invented the material is hoping it will eventually be used to heat car seats. While electrified printer ink may still be a ways off, you could one day own a T-shirt with your favorite electronics embedded in the fabric.

Conductors and insulators make life more convenient and safe, and will probably keep amazing us with new uses for a long time to come.

One day your car seat may be coated with a substance you can choose to heat.

Glossary

atom   The basic unit of matter made up of a nucleus and negatively (–) charged electrons

conductor   A material that electricity can easily pass through

corrode   To break down through chemical reaction

current   Flowing electrons

electrical arc   A current moving between two conductors through a gas

filament   The conducting wire in a light bulb

generator   A machine that produces an electrical current

insulator   A material that electricity cannot pass through

ion   A charged (+ or –) particle

lightning rod   A rod that conducts lightning into the ground

microchip   A wafer of semiconducting material containing circuitry

molecules   Many atoms together

ohm   A unit of measure of a material's resistance to current

oxidize   To change chemcially because of being exposed to oxygen

resistance   A material's opposition to electrical current

semiconductor   A material that can conduct and resist the flow of electrical current

static   An electrical charge (+ or –) on an object

superconductor   A material that has no resistance to the flow of electrical current

third rail   The rail that acts as a conductor, supplying electricity to trains and subways

vacuum   The absence of matter

Learning More

FURTHER READING

Hydroelectric Power: Power from Moving Water (Energy Revolution). Marguerite Rodger. Crabtree Publishing, 2010.

Inventing the Electric Light (Breakthrough Inventions). Lisa Mullins. Crabtree Publishing, 2007.

Using Energy (Green Team). Sally Hewitt. Crabtree Publishing, 2008.

What Is Electricity? (Understanding Electricity). Ronald Monroe. Crabtree Publishing, 2012.

What Are Electrical Circuits? (Understanding Electricity). Ronald Monroe. Crabtree Publishing, 2012.

What Is Electromagnetism? (Understanding Electricity). Lionel Sandner. Crabtree Publishing, 2012.

WEBSITES

NASA, Understanding Electricity
http://scifiles.larc.nasa.gov/kids/Problem_Board/problems/electricity/electricity2.html

Fun with Electricity
www.jea.com/community/education/kidscorner/electricalfacts.asp

Kids Korner, Conductors and Insulators
www.fplsafetyworld.com/?ver=kkblue&utilid=www.fplsafetyworld.com&id=16185

Manitoba Hydro Electric Universe
http://manitoba.electricuniverse.com/

Science Kids, Circuits and Conductors
www.sciencekids.co.nz/gamesactivities/circuitsconductors.html

Index